The Richest Treasure

The

The Warmth, Joy, and Inspiration
Of Friendship in the Words of
Famous Men and Women

Richest

Selected by Marianne Wilson
and Paul Montgomery

Treasure

HALLMARK EDITIONS

The Richest Treasure

Friends Are Like Flowers

Friends are like flowers.
I have found them so:
The hardy staunch perennials that grow
Year after year are like
some friends I know.

One need not cultivate them with great care,
They only need the sun and wind and air
Of trust and love,
and they are always there.

Some must be nursed with frequent
trowel and spade,
And sheltered from the sun
or too much shade,
For fear their frail and clinging bloom
may fade.

Friends are like flowers.
I would be a friend
Whose blossomings no hand need ever tend:
A perennial on whom hearts can depend.

GRACE NOLL CROWELL

Laughter and Friends

"Laughter is better when friends laugh together"
writes "Quintus Quiz" in this "Letter to the Edi-
tor" of the Christian Century. *He emphasizes*
how pleasurable laughter is when it is shared
with friends:

Laughter is better when friends laugh together.
For laughter demands for its full exercise what
only friends can give. When we laugh together,
we implicitly declare that we share certain be-
liefs and principles. We accept the same general
substructure of life; we could not see the incon-
gruous if we did not have some common idea of
what is congruous and befitting, for much of our
laughter has its source in surprise and contrast.

Again, laughter demands the complete trust
of those who share it with us. There must be no
suspicion. We must not stand upon ceremony.
We certainly must not be prigs, watching jeal-
ously for any breach of what seem the eternal
conventions. If we are extravagant or absurd or
ridiculous we expect our friends to understand us.

You must call to mind hours which your friend
and you spent in conversation in which you
went deep down to the very springs of life—and
how merrily you laughed. Nothing goes better
with the real spiritual life than mirth. I have a

dear friend who tells the story that he and I were once requested to leave a tea shop because of our excessive laughter. We had been discussing with great delight the doctrine of the Trinity, for which both of us had and still have a profound faith and love. And why not? It is rightly said that no one really believes fully in anything until he is prepared to be merry about it. "Him serve with mirth"—that is the right reading.

Both are good things—laughter and the love of friends. And what God has joined together, let no man put asunder. Ever yours, hoping to laugh with you again.

Community of Man

The modern French writer Antoine de Saint-Exupéry, author of The Little Prince *and* Wind, Sand, and Stars, *was a flyer before and during World War II. This experience led to his increased awareness of personal relationships with men of all nationalities:*

In my civilization, he who is different from me does not impoverish me—he enriches me. Our unity is constituted in something higher than ourselves—in Man. When we of Group 2-33 argue of an evening, our arguments do not strain our fraternity, they reenforce it. For no man seeks to hear his own echo, or to find his reflection in the glass. Staring into the glass called Man, the Frenchman of France sees the Norwegian of Norway; for Man heightens and absorbs them both, finds room in himself for the customs of the French as easily as for the manners of the Norwegians. Tales of snow are told in Norway, tulips are grown in Holland, flamencos are sung in Spain—and we, participating in Man, are enriched by them all.

Faults

They came to tell your faults to me,
They named them over one by one;
I laughed aloud when they were done,
I knew them all so well before,—
Oh, they were blind, too blind to see
Your faults had made me love you more.

SARA TEASDALE

To be capable of steady friendship
and lasting love, are the two greatest proofs,
not only of goodness of heart,
but of strength of mind.   WILLIAM HAZLITT

Friendship is the gift of the gods, and the most precious boon to man.   BENJAMIN DISRAELI

A Good Friend Is a Rich Treasure

An eleventh-century Persian prince named Kai Kā'ūs wrote a guidebook called A Mirror for Princes *in order to instruct his young son in deportment. In this selection, he advises his son in the art of making and keeping friends:*

He who never spares a thought for friends never has them. Form the habit, therefore, of making friends with all manner of persons; many of man's faults are hidden from his friends, although his virtues are revealed to them.

When you find new friends, never turn your back on old ones and so you will always possess a host of them; and there is a saying that a good friend is a rich treasure. Give a thought also to the people who are advancing towards friendship with you but are only quasi-friends, to whom you should make yourself well-disposed and affable, agreeing with them in all matters good or bad and showing yourself to be favorably inclined towards them. In that manner, experiencing nothing but civility from you, they become wholeheartedly your friends. When Alexander

9

was asked by virtue of what it was that he had been able to acquire so great an empire in so short a space of time, he replied, "By winning over enemies by kindliness and gathering friends about me by solicitude for them."

St. Valentine's Day

Faith Baldwin's name is synonymous with inspiration. Her books have charmed and uplifted many readers. She writes about friendship, "that warmth and reassurance which is from the heart" in this selection from her book Testament of Trust:

Now, in New England [in February] we bundle up, eyes, ears, feet, but the heart can be worn on the sleeve if you want to risk it. It's the season of hearts and flowers (even if they bloom under the sheltered south window), so hearts are trumps. *Tête-à-tête* is a pleasant, common phrase for confidential conversation but "heart-to-heart" is a better one. No matter what one is saying aloud, we know at times that human spirits speak silently to one another.

What a wonderful word heart is and capable of how many interpretations! We sign ourselves to someone we love, "with all my heart"; we speak, when sorrowful, of "a heavy heart"; we remark, when we're doing something without pleasure, "My heart's not in it."...

When we sit with friends and speak of a trouble uppermost in our minds, we are easing our hearts, and when we are grateful beyond any word for the answered prayer or the strong arm in time of distress, we say, our hearts overflow.... So it's not all written on the valentines, which 'according to custom' we open on the fourteenth....

When we obey unconsciously the admonition to let our light so shine, it is the light of the heart as well as of the soul. I know this when a friend comes into the room saying nothing unusual yet bearing with him, or her, that warmth and reassurance which is from the heart and is indeed a light.

A good mathematician may know the truth about numbers, and a good engineer may know how to make physical forces serve his purposes. But the engineer and the mathematician are human beings first—so for them, as well as for me, what matters most is not one's knowledge and skill, but one's relations with other people.

ARNOLD TOYNBEE

11

Part of God's Plan

What made us friends in the long ago

When first we met?

Well I think I know;

The best in me and the best in you

Hailed each other because they knew

That always and always

since life began

Our being friends was part of God's plan.

GEORGE WEBSTER DOUGLAS

A Rare and Wonderful Fellowship

In her book A Man Called Peter, *Catherine Marshall writes about her warm experiences with her husband Peter Marshall—Presbyterian minister and United States Senate chaplain. In this selection from that book, Mrs. Marshall describes her late husband's fun-loving friends, recalling that "underneath all the fun, they had the greatest respect and affection for one another":*

The "gang" was made up of five ministers, from a variety of denominations, each pastor of one of Washington's large downtown churches. Dr. Anderson, of First Congregational, was a sort of ecclesiastical Bob Hope to the group. It was impossible to be overly serious when Howard was around, and any ministerial stuffiness was immediately punctured. There was Dr. John Rustin, nicknamed by the group "pack-'em-in-Rustin," because John always dealt in large numbers. There was Oscar (Dr. Blackwelder), of the Lutheran Church of the Reformation, whom they called "Sun-crowned Oscar" because of a favorite sermon he preached called "Sun-crowned Men"; and "Cranny"—Dr. Clarence W. Cranford —of Calvary Baptist. Dr. Edward Pruden, of First Baptist, later President Truman's pastor, was another charter member. Ed, they called, "Peace-at-any-price-Pruden," and Ed grinned and bore it. Peter was known as "Twittering-birds Marshall" because of the poetic imagery for which his sermons were famous.

The fellowship between these men was rare and wonderful. They had all come to Washington at about the same time. There was complete frankness, much letting down of the hair, and much levity. But underneath all the fun, they had the greatest respect and affection for one another and the prodigious job that each man was doing. There were deep and lasting bonds between them. To this day, each man cherishes the memories of their group friendship as one of the richest and most unforgettable experiences of his life. . . .

One year, on April 1st, a union service was to be held at noon in the First Congregational Church. Several of the ministers had parts in the service; Peter had been delegated to preach. At five minutes to twelve, while the men waited in Dr. Anderson's study, a Western Union messenger knocked on the door and delivered a telegram to Peter. He read it, and his mouth dropped open.

"Is anything the matter?" asked Cranny.

Peter sat there, turning the yellow sheet over and over, as if hunting for some clue. Then he handed it to Dr. Cranford. "Read it. Read it out loud, so the others can hear."

ALL IS DISCOVERED FLEE

A FRIEND

The "gang" promptly accused Howard of being the culprit, but he vigorously denied it. The identity of the April-fool prankster was never discovered.

Stories about Dr. Anderson could be multiplied *ad infinitum.* He was irrepressible. One day he was presiding at an interdenominational ministers' meeting held in the Cleveland Park Congregational Church. Dr. Anderson was in the midst of delivering a quite serious talk. Peter came in late, and finding the church well filled, was forced to take a seat in the front row. Just as he got seated—unobtrusively, he hoped—Howard interrupted himself suddenly, leaned far over the pulpit, and stared at Peter. There was a long, awkward silence broken by Howard's saying in a resounding voice, "And who is this sinner come to justice?" The laughter that followed almost broke up the meeting.

Fellowship in joy, not sympathy in sorrow, is what makes friends.

FRIEDRICH NIETZSCHE

Kindred Spirits

Famous French author André Maurois, whose books have been popular in both French- and English-speaking countries for many years, compares love and friendship in this selection from his well-known book, The Art of Living:

In the early stages it [friendship] seems such a fragile plant that love, springing up close to its pale, weak stalk, may smother it. La Rochefoucauld says that most women are little given to friendship, because friendship is insipid compared to love. Insipid? No, but cruelly lucid in its early stages. Titania's blindness does not affect those who are seeking friendship; for them an ass's head is an ass's head. And how could one love a person with an ass's head? How is the close bond of friendship to be established between two perfectly lucid people who are not physically attracted to one another?

In some cases this close bond is entirely natural, for the very simple reason that the person encountered possesses rare qualities that are recognized as such. There is friendship at first sight as well as love. A word, a smile, a look reveals a kindred spirit. A charming act makes us sure we have discovered a noble personality. So friendship starts with friendship as love starts with love. These sudden friendships are possible even when the chosen friend does not possess high qualities, for all discrimination is relative. One young girl suddenly becomes the confidante and constant companion of another; by still another she is thoroughly disliked. In the first instance, chance has revealed a kind of pre-established harmony and friendship comes into being....

A chance word or look, then, may reveal similarity in personality and intelligence. Restraint and willpower allow this early sympathy to grow and establish itself. Confidences are exchanged and we soon achieve far more intellectual freedom with this comparative stranger than with those to whom we are bound by ties of blood or physical love.

Are new friends who are worthy of friendship, to be preferred to old friends? The question is unworthy of a human being, for there should be no surfeit of friendships as there is of other things; and, as in the case of wines that improve with age, the oldest friendships ought to be the most delightful; moreover, the well-known adage is true: "Men must eat many a peck of salt together before the claims of friendship are fulfilled." CICERO

Finding the Gentleness to Love

The late Thomas Merton, a Trappist monk and priest, wrote more than thirty books, including the best-selling autobiography, The Seven Storey Mountain. *Like Anne Morrow Lindbergh, Thomas Merton believed that periods of personal solitude heighten the joy of friendship:*

It is in deep solitude that I find the gentleness with which I can truly love my brothers. The more solitary I am, the more affection I have for them. It is pure affection, and filled with reverence for the solitude of others. Solitude and silence teach me to love my brothers for what they are, not for what they say. Now it is no longer a question of dishonoring them by accepting their fictions, believing in their images of themselves which their weakness obliges them to compose, in the wan work of communication. Yet there will, it is true, always remain a dialectic between the words of men and their being. This will tell something about them we would not have realized if the words had not been there.

19

Memory

Memory, like tapestry,

        Sets forth in colors gay

The hopes, the dreams, the happiness

        That blessed our yesterday.

Golden threads for golden deeds,

        Rosy tints for dreams come true;

For friendships earned and friendships held

        Are tints of heavenly blue.

RUTH CRAVEN

Memories to Treasure

The story of Helen Keller is the story of a woman's magnificent struggle with and mastery over blindness. Her humanitarianism pervades this selection from her book The Open Door:

If there were no life beyond this earth-life, some people I have known would gain immortality by the nobility of our memory of them. With every friend I love who has been taken into the brown bosom of the earth a part of me has been buried there; but their contribution of happiness, strength, and understanding to my being remains to sustain me in an altered world.

I am too happy in this world to think much about the future, except to remember that I have cherished friends awaiting me there in God's beautiful somewhere. In spite of the lapse of years, they seem so close to me that I should not think it strange if at any moment they should clasp my hand and speak words of endearment as they used to before they went away.

It has been said that life has treated me harshly; and sometimes I have complained in my heart because many pleasures of human experience have been withheld from me, but when I recollect the treasure of friendship that has been bestowed on me I withdraw all charges against life. If much has been denied me, much, very much has been given me. So long as the memory of certain beloved friends lives in my heart I shall say that life is good.

Deepening Friendships

In her book, Women in Wonderland, *Dorothy Dohen gives some thoughtful tips on preserving friendship throughout "all the changes and vicissitudes of the friends' lives":*

Obviously it takes two to make a friendship just as it takes two to make a quarrel, and obviously, too, it takes two to keep a friendship. But in any human relationship, one cannot measure the extent of one's giving. Women must be aware of a pettiness that can take the edge of joy off a friendship. ("She didn't remember my birthday so I won't remember hers." "She always expects me to phone her and she never phones me." And so on.) While, as Cicero remarked, it is the essence of true friendship that it should be immortal, nevertheless, one has to work at keeping one's friends. A true friendship can persist even when one goes off to a cloister and the other stays in the world, or one gets married and the other remains single, provided both friends are willing to make the necessary adjustments. The single woman who expects her friend who marries to be able to spend as much time with her as she did formerly is herself the cause of the destruction of the friendship. In friendship, as in everything human, there is inevitable change, for one cannot grow unless one changes. So, while both growth and change can be painful they are usually to be welcomed. A friendship to be preserved over the years, through all the changes and vicissitudes of the friends' lives, must be adjusted and readjusted. If both friends realize this, their friendship can deepen as it progresses.

Friendship needs no words—it is a loneliness relieved of the anguish of loneliness.

DAG HAMMARSKJÖLD

Some imagine that friendship is an affair of continual meetings. This is not so; it is a frank exchange of confidence, a sense of comprehension and response which may last a lifetime, transcending space and time.   A. J. CRONIN

24

There is a world of difference between the mass gregariousness which has for so long been the admired hallmark of American "friendliness" and the real deep sustained emotions of friendship.

MARYA MANNES

The Three of Us

Gladys Taber, author of the popular Stillmeadow Farm books, writes here of her unusual friendship with Hazel, Ted Key's cartoon character, and Ted Key himself:

My friend Hazel, who lives with Ted Key, sent me a picture of herself this week with four dogs. I sometimes think the reason I love Ted Key so much is that Hazel is so much like me. More dynamic, true, this stocky arbiter of the house, but Hazel and I are kin just the same. I would never ask Ted how he dreamed Hazel up for the cartoons that have enchanted the country for so long in the *Post* and in books, for that would be to admit Hazel is invented and this I could never admit. When I get a letter from Hazel, it is from Hazel and no other. If I have anything to say to Ted, I write it on another piece of paper and address it to him. Now and then he himself sends me a note. But usually just a message through

Hazel, or a postscript saying simply. "Me too. Ted."

We have a lovely three-way friendship and we are all perfectly happy with it, but I can well imagine some people might find it a little odd. For one thing, neither Ted nor Hazel has ever visited me nor I them. And if Ted came with his family, wife and boys, how would he ever explain to me that Hazel had been left at home? I dare say it is bad enough when one artist has an alter ego but when someone else gets the same one too, it is quite strange. Anyhow, I noted that Hazel's latest picture to me was of her, four-square and solid, with a cocker in her lap and an Irish peering over her shoulder and two more just dogs around her lap too.

My dogs, really.

Recently Ted had a *Post* cartoon with a little frustrated man looking dismally at a very large dog, obviously Irish, sitting on a sofa. Fresh paint all over sofa, dog and all chairs in the room.

I flew to the post office to send an urgent message to Hazel that I could not live without that picture. And Hazel wrote back that she was sending the jerk right over to the magazine office to get the original back, OR ELSE. When it came, a small note by Ted on the bottom said, "Better just paint everything the same yellow!"

Yellow was, of course, the color the Irish had tracked over everything.

I now have quite a gallery of Hazel, via Ted. Including the one with a whole house jammed with Easter chicks and Hazel saying firmly, "Watch Your Step!"

I suppose the reason Ted Key is such a fine artist is that he has a warm heart, a sensitivity combined with his feeling that life is pretty funny if you look at it from the right angle. I do not know if he feels this, as my letters to Hazel are on a different plane, naturally. Hazel isn't interested in art, just in running that family.

Parted friends coming in contact at long intervals are like the characters of a play, the living drama maintains its interest at every reappearance.   WILLIAM BELL SCOTT

Old friends are the great blessing of one's latter years. Half a word conveys one's meaning. They have a memory of the same events, and have the same mode of thinking. I have young relations that may grow upon me, for my nature is affectionate, but can they grow old friends?

                              HORACE WALPOLE

Small Service

Small service is true service while it lasts;

Of friends, however humble, scorn not one;

The daisy by the shadow that it casts

Protects the lingering dewdrop from the sun.

WILLIAM WORDSWORTH

'Our Ideals of Friendship'

Inspired by the words of Emerson, "A friend is one who makes us be our best," author Anne Bryan McCall points out how friendship can become "a higher and lovelier thing":

In youth we set up standards of our own. The schoolmate who prefers us to others, she is our friend; or the one who listens most sympathetically while we talk of ourselves; or the one who defends us against our enemies; or the one most in need of our friendship and whom we defend.

Yet these are but very personal and individual standards, and of little final worth. As we grow older we find less and less of the personal in our ideals of friendship, and more and more of the general. We find friendship not to be a mere relation between ourselves and some beloved fellow creature, but a large and noble ideal still to be enjoyed and attained by noble and high natures, even should we, by folly or misfortune, fail of it altogether.

It is this high general ideal of friendship, this high standard that must be little by little learned and conformed to, if we are to have true friendship in our lives.

But I believe we shall best come at high standards of friendship by a study of the usually very faulty personal standards which so many of us employ.

One of the most common personal standards that we employ requires that our friends shall always and without fail approve of us. Approval, devotion, demonstration of affection, these we require, insist on. What burning bitterness and hurt-of-heart often arise when our friends fall short of this, our personal standard.

But now hear what Emerson says of friendship. He is not setting down any personal ideal, mind you, but a very high and general one. He says: "A friend is one who makes us be our best."

How far it all is from petty quarrels, petty fault-findings, differences of opinion and misunderstandings.

Emerson does not say in just what ways a friend "makes us be our best." That, no doubt, is a matter of varying circumstance. But if you examine his ideal carefully, you will find a double obligation. Our friend by his own noble means expects and requires and obliges us to be our noblest and best; and—now note this—*we meet that obligation.* On one side is a high and noble ideal, and expectation of the "best" that is in us; and on the other side a recognition of that ideal and a fulfilling of it.

Morning Prayer

Let me today do something that shall take
    A little sadness from the world's vast store,
    And may I be so favored as to make
        Of joy's too scanty sum a little more.
Let me not hurt, by any selfish deed
        Or thoughtless word,
            the heart of foe or friend;
        Nor would I pass, unseeing, worthy need,
    Or sin by silence when I should defend.
However meager be my worldly wealth
    Let me give something that shall aid my kind,
A word of courage, or a thought of health,
    Dropped as I pass for troubled hearts to find.
Let me tonight look back across the span
        'Twixt dawn and dark,
            and to my conscience say—
    Because of some good act to beast or man—
        "The world is better that I lived today."

ELLA WHEELER WILCOX

Extending the Circle

Popular novelist A. J. Cronin joins the plea for varied friendships in his essay, "A Thousand and One Lives." Here he quotes famous men whose friendships were extensive:

Some of us travel through life on a conducted tour, making friends only with the people inside the bus, keeping to the main roads and recognized centers. Then we realize too late that our lives are narrow, and complain that we are not fully living—forgetful of the fact that the remedy lies in our own hands. If we are willing to go off the beaten track, to make friends and acquaintances with people of diverse callings, we shall find our lives immeasurably enriched. In the words of the Arab proverb, "Let a man make varied friends and he will lead a thousand and one lives."

Ever since Aristotle, philosophers have agreed that even more than health or great talents a plenitude of friends is the greatest good in life. Yet, while this lies wholly within our power to secure, how seldom is it used as a working principle in daily life! Few of us really try to extend the circle of our acquaintances in the spirit of Samuel Johnson, who said, "I look upon every day as lost in which I do not make a new acquaintance." Dr. Johnson's friends, as in the case of most men who have had full and rewarding careers, were in all walks of life, for he realized that no one can claim to know life until he knows all types of men.

It is easier than we think to strike up a friendship. Whenever he entered a shop, Daniel Webster used to start a conversation with the storekeeper, asking a question about a fine point involved in the shopkeeper's trade: in grinding coffee, for instance, or selecting a choice cigar. He knew that few people can resist discoursing on a subject in which they are expert; once the ice had been broken in this way he found that other exchanges followed easily and naturally.

Some imagine that friendship is an affair of continual meetings. This is not so; it is a frank exchange of confidence, a sense of comprehension and response which may last a lifetime, transcending space and time. No one led a more remote life than David Livingstone, the explorer, yet he had countless friends. His youngest daughter said of him: "I remember him as always writing letters." He sent hundreds each year to friends all over the world, many of whom he knew only from a chance and fleeting acquaintance.

To declare that we already have a few old friends, neighbors and business associates and that life does not allow for more is a mistaken view. Nothing is more limiting than a closed circle of acquaintanceship where every avenue of conversation has been explored and social exchanges are fixed in a known routine. Sir William Osler used to say, "A man starts to grow old when he stops making new friends. For this is the sign of development, of assimilating new ideas, of zest for life."

And whatever else a friend may be, she is never a bore to her friend. You like her because she is she and you are you. JESSAMYN WEST

The Highest Loyalty

"If I had to choose between betraying my country and betraying my friend, I hope I should have the guts to betray my country." In this selection from his well-known book Two Cheers for Democracy, *British novelist E. M. Forster explains why he believes friendship deserves man's highest priority:*
Starting from them [personal relationships] I get a little order into the contemporary chaos. One must be fond of people and trust them if one is

not to make a mess of life, and it is therefore essential that they should not let one down. They often do. The moral of which is that I must, myself, be as reliable as possible, and this I try to be. But reliability is not a matter of contract—that is the main difference between the world of personal relationships and the world of business relationships. It is a matter for the heart, which signs no documents. In other words, reliability is impossible unless there is a natural warmth. Most men possess this warmth, though they often have bad luck and get chilled. Most of them, even when they are politicians, *want* to keep faith. And one can, at all events, show one's own little light here, one's own poor little trembling flame, with the knowledge that it is not the only light that is shining in the darkness, and not the only one which the darkness does not comprehend.

Personal relations are despised today. They are regarded as bourgeois luxuries, as products of a time of fair weather which is now past, and we are urged to get rid of them, and to dedicate ourselves to some movement or cause instead. I hate the idea of causes, and if I had to choose between betraying my country and betraying my friend, I hope I should have the guts to betray my country. Such a choice may scandalize the modern reader, and he may stretch out his patriotic hand to the telephone at once and ring up the police. It would not have shocked Dante, though. Dante places Brutus and Cassius in the lowest circle of Hell because they had chosen to betray their friend Julius Caesar rather than their country Rome.

Probably one will not be asked to make such an agonizing choice. Still, there lies at the back of every creed something terrible and hard for which the worshipper may one day be required to suffer, and there is even a terror and a hardness in this creed of personal relationships, urbane and mild though it sounds. Love and loyalty to an individual can run counter to the claims of the State. When they do—down with the State, say I, which means that the State would down me.

It takes patience sometimes to appreciate the true values in the people with whom circumstances have surrounded us. It takes awareness to recognize these values when they appear.... Aren't friendships, on whatever level, a part of human fortune? Friendships can be infinitely varied. And by their very differentness the whole pattern of one's days can be enlivened, and in so many ways rewarding.   MARJORIE HOLMES

'A Thousand Times More Sweet'

Henry van Dyke, a prolific writer, gained immense popularity in the United States shortly after the turn of the century. His books are warm and inspiring as is this selection about friendship from Fisherman's Luck:

But after all, the very best thing in good talk, and the thing that helps it most, is *friendship.* How it dissolves the barriers that divide us, and loosens all constraint, and diffuses itself like some fine old cordial through all the veins of life—this feeling that we understand and trust each other, and wish each other heartily well! Everything into which it really comes is good. It transforms letter-writing from a task into a pleasure. It makes music a thousand times more sweet. The people who play and sing not *at* us, but *to* us,—how delightful it is to listen to them! Yes, there is a talkability that can express itself without words. There is an exchange of thought and feeling which is happy alike in speech and in silence. It is quietness pervaded with friendship.

Treasure is not always a friend but a friend is always a treasure.   RUSSIAN PROVERB

A Smile Is a Light

A smile is a light in the window
                        of a face that signifies
        The heart is at home and waiting.
Nothing on earth can smile but man.
                Gems may flash reflective light,
                        but what is the flash of a diamond
        Compared with a flash of a smile?
A face that cannot smile is like
                        a bud that cannot blossom.
        It withers and dies on its stalk.
Laughter is day. Sobriety is night.
                And the smile is the twilight
                        That hovers gently between both,
                More bewitching than either.

                        HENRY WARD BEECHER

To Sow With Love

And a youth said, Speak to us of Friendship.
    And he answered, saying:
    Your friend is your needs answered.
    He is your field which you sow with love
and reap with thanksgiving.
    And he is your board and your fireside.
    For you come to him with your hunger,
and you seek him for peace.
    When your friend speaks his mind
you fear not the "nay" in your own mind,
nor do you withhold the "ay."
    And when he is silent your heart ceases not
to listen to his heart;
    For without words, in friendship,
all thoughts, all desires,
all expectations are born and shared,
with joy that is unacclaimed.
    When you part from your friend,
you grieve not;
    For that which you love most in him
may be clearer in his absence,
as the mountain to the climber
is clearer from the plain.

And let there be no purpose in friendship
save the deepening of the spirit.

For love that seeks aught but the disclosure
of its own mystery is not love but a net cast
forth: and only the unprofitable is caught.

And let your best be for your friend.

If he must know the ebb of your tide,
let him know its flood also.

For what is your friend that you
should seek him with hours to kill?

Seek him always with hours to live.

For it is his to fill your need,
but not your emptiness.

And in the sweetness of friendship let there
be laughter, and sharing of pleasures.

For in the dew of little things the heart
finds its morning and is refreshed.

KAHLIL GIBRAN

Friendship

Friendship needs no symbol,

Or vow to make it whole;

It's just a sacred covenant

That's locked within the soul;

It knows no creed or station,

Or thought of gain or fame,

For what it does is sacred,

And is done in Friendship's name.

EMILY R. GRAY

'A Different Theory'

Pulitzer-prize winning author Phyllis McGinley writes about home and family life, often with a light touch of wry wit. In this selection from her book The Province of the Heart, *she is convincing in her "theory" that friendship between women* does *exist, despite popular opinion to the contrary:*

Although the story goes that woman was contrived from Adam's rib, I have a different theory. In her public sense, she sprang full-panoplied out of his imagination. For centuries woman battened on male illusion, finding she was cherished in direct proportion to how well she lived up to her myth. Even today, with medicine and sociology chipping away at our legend so that we are in danger of losing much of our armor and a good deal of allure, certain misconceptions linger. We find it useful to foster them. So I hope I won't be read out of the party if I smash one more masculine belief—the belief that women dislike other women.

For quite the contrary is true. Women like other women fine. The more feminine she is, the more comfortable a woman feels with her own sex. It is only the occasional and therefore noticeable adventuress who refuses to make friends with us. (I speak now of genuine friendship. Our love we reserve for its proper object, man.)

Watch women at cocktail parties. All eyes and smiles for the gentlemen at first, the safe (by which I mean the satisfactorily married) ladies begin gradually to drift away from the bantering males. They do it tactfully. The fiction must be maintained that men are their sole concern. But by almost imperceptible degrees women edge toward some sofa where another woman is ensconced. There, while the talk seethes and bubbles around them, they whisper cozily together of truly important things like baby-sitters and little dressmakers.

Do I imply by this that women are as frivolous and unintellectual as they have been accused of being in other eras? Or that the larger issues do not concern them? Far from it. I am simply trying to convey the natural attraction that binds us together. Those two women on the sofa might well go on from household problems to the lesser topics of literature, space rockets, or politics. I know. For I am frequently one of the ladies on the sofa. In other words, I like women.

My reasons are many and sufficient. I like them for their all-around, all-weather dependability. I like them because they are generally so steady, realistic, and careful about tidying up after a hot shower. I admire them for their prudence, thrift, gallantry, common sense, and knobless knees, and because they are neither so vain nor so given to emotion as their opposite numbers. I like the way they answer letters promptly, put shoe trees in their shoes at night, and are so durable physically. Their natures may not be so fine or their hearts so readily touched as man's, but they are not so easily imposed on either. I respect them, too, because they are so good at handling automobiles.

Dedicatory Ode

They say that in the unchanging place,
   Where all we loved is always dear,
We meet our morning face to face
   And find at last our twentieth year...
They say (and I am glad they say)
   It is so; and it may be so:
It may be just the other way,
   I cannot tell. But this I know:
From quiet homes and first beginning,
   Out to the undiscovered ends,
There's nothing worth the wear of winning,
   But laughter and the love of friends.

HILAIRE BELLOC

If a man does not make new acquaintances as he advances through life, he will soon find himself left alone. A man, Sir, should keep his friendships in constant repair. SAMUEL JOHNSON

The Gold of Friendship

Marjorie Holmes, whose warm and human book, Love and Laughter, *has delighted thousands of readers, turns her attention to friendship in this selection from that book. Here she writes:"If you truly love and enjoy your friends they are a part of the golden circlet that makes life good.":*

It was a party, in the truest sense of the word. An assortment of interesting people, small enough so that strangers could become acquainted, old friends could talk. Yet large enough to be full of laughter and music and pleasantries and stimulating new contacts.

On impulse I remarked to our hostess, Peg Howe: "You certainly have . . . lovely friends."

"Oh, yes," she laughed. And lifting her braceleted arm she remarked, "My friends are the charms on my bracelet of life."

The charms! I thought. Why—yes. The enhancements, the adornments—that extra shining something. If you truly love and enjoy your

49

friends they are a part of the golden circlet that makes life good.

When you gather them about you, you feel happy—and proud. Their accomplishments add a glow to your own being. What's more, you want to share them: "He's a distinguished surgeon, and his wife makes a home for all these foreign students—you must meet them."..."They both do little theater work, you'll just love them, they're both so alive—"..."He plays folk songs on the guitar and sings in three languages—"... "Now that the children are in school she's studying law."...

But not only their accomplishments, their qualities: "Helen is the most generous person I've ever known."..."Grace has the most beautiful brown eyes—when she talks they just shine—"..."Jim has a laugh that makes you feel good all over. And you can depend on what he says, he'd never let you down—"

The person who can feel and speak this way about his friends is truly blessed. His life is rich in meaningful relationships. His "friends" are not a source of criticism and carping and jealousy and gossip. They are people truly dear to him, so dear that he can't refrain from singing their praises to others. And in so doing he is always making new ones. For the way a person feels about his friends is a pretty accurate indication of the kind of person he or she is.

The man or woman who treasures his friends is usually solid gold himself.

I am singularly rich in friendships. Friends of all ages have contributed enormously to my happiness and helped me greatly in times of need. I learned one of the great secrets of friendship early in life—to regard each person with whom one associates as an end in himself, not a means to one's own ends.   CARROLL BINDER

Everybody in the world, little and big, has one *special* friend, a friend that he's *glad* to do favors for—not sour about it, but *glad*—glad clear to the marrow. And so, I don't care where you start, you can get at anybody's ear that you want to— I don't care how low you are, nor how high he is. And it's so simple: you've only to find the *first* friend, that is all; that ends your part of the work. He finds the next friend himself, and that one finds the third, and so on, friend after friend, link after link, like a chain; and you can go up it or down it, as high as you like or as low as you like.   MARK TWAIN

Old Friendship

Beautiful and rich is an old friendship,

Grateful to the touch as ancient ivory,

Smooth as aged wine, or sheen of tapestry

Where light has lingered,

intimate and long.

Full of tears and warm is an old friendship

That asks no longer deeds of gallantry,

Or any deed at all—

save that the friend shall be

Alive and breathing somewhere, like a song.

EUNICE TIETJENS

When Friends Are Friendlier

Just as people differ, so do friendships. Humorist Don Marquis, whose Archy and Mehitabel are among the most famous friends of modern literature, describes one of his more unusual friendships and then adds some thoughts on friendship in general:

A cross-grained, long-nosed fellow, with a tongue as sharp as a new-whetted carving knife, has long been my unspared and unsparing friend.

We have quarreled every time we have met for years; quarreled about anything and everything and nothing. He rams home devastating truths about my character, and twists them in the wound. I like him because I can be myself with him, for he can take the truth as well as give it.

Once when I heard he was very ill, I wrote him a letter on the advantages of dying and getting it over with, instead of dragging along and tiring everybody out with the graceless process. This so enraged him that his blood started circulating again, and he got well. Once when I was very ill, and "busted" on top of that, he and a couple of others got hold of quite a lump of money—stole it, for all I know—and sent it to me with an insulting message.

54

Our friendship has survived both insults and benefits, neglect and obligation. Benefits should be exchanged between friends upon occasion, and then forgotten on both sides; benefits are often harder to forgive than injuries, if the consciousness of them remains with either party.

Pity, even with apparent cause, is the ultimate hurt, for it corrodes the soul. And true friendship presupposes self-respect, as well as respect for one's friend.

You will find, at times, that some friend has sloughed you off, as if you were so much dandruff. But there is nothing for you to regret when this happens. It may result from causes totally unrelated to friendship. It may be due to a healthy growth on one side, or on both, but divergent in direction, and not to any deterioration in character or to any betrayal.

Many of my friends are far more friendly when all is fair weather with me. This is natural, and carries no reproach with it. When one is successful and happy he radiates an atmosphere which is attractive. When he has permitted a defeat, or a success, to make him glum, people get fed up with him, and rightly.

In friendship, as in other relationships, you take out what you put in.

The Voice of a Friend

God speaks to us in the gentle rain

    That splashes and taps on our windowpane;

We hear His voice in the comforting sigh

    Of the wind as it goes murmuring by,

In the roar of the sea and the song of birds

    We hear the majesty of His words,

    And when silent nights

        wear a star-studded crown

God talks in a language transcending all sound;

    But His message of hope

        and love without end

Is most clearly heard in the voice of a friend.

DEAN WALLEY

What friends do with us and for us is a real part of our life; for it strengthens and advances our personality. The assault of our enemies is not part of our life; it is only part of our experience; we throw it off and guard ourselves against it as against frost, storm, rain, hail, or any other of the external evils which may be expected to happen.

GOETHE

'Friendship Is Evanescent'

Best known for his classic Walden, *Henry David Thoreau also published a number of poems and a journal of a week-long river trip. In this selection from that journal, Thoreau uses the example of the elements of nature to define friendship:* WEDNESDAY: While we float here, far from that tributary stream on whose banks our friends and kindred dwell, our thoughts, like the stars, come out of their horizon still. After years of vain familiarity, some distant gesture or unconscious behavior, which we remember, speaks to us with more emphasis than the wisest or kindest words. We are sometimes made aware of a kindness long passed, and realize that there have been times when our friends' thoughts of us were of so pure and lofty a character that they passed over us like the winds of heaven un-noticed; when they treated us not as what we were, but as what we aspired to be. Friendship is evanescent in every man's experience, and re-membered like heat lightning in past summers. Fair and flitting like a summer cloud—there is always some vapor in the air, no matter how long the drought.

My friends are my estate. Forgive me then the avarice to hoard them! They tell me those who were poor early have different views of gold. I don't know how that is. God is not so wary as we, else He would give us no friends, lest we forget Him! The charms of the heaven in the bush are superseded, I fear, by the heaven in the hand occasionally.

EMILY DICKINSON

INDEX

Set in Trump Mediaeval, a Venetian face designed by
Professor Georg Trump of Munich, Germany.
Set at Huxley House Ltd.
Printed on Hallmark Eggshell Book paper.
Designed by Trudi Boese.